DATE DUE

Yellow Umbrella Books are published by Red Brick Learning
7825 Telegraph Road, Bloomington, Minnesota 55438
http://www.redbricklearning.com

Library of Congress Cataloging-in-Publication Data
Bauer, David (David S.)
    [Signs. Spanish & English]
    Signs/by David Bauer = Señales y rótulos/por David Bauer
    p. cm.
    Includes index.
    Summary: "Simple text and photos introduce some examples of common
environmental print, such as a stop sign"—Provided by publisher.
    ISBN-13: 978-0-7368-6025-3 (hardcover)
    ISBN-10: 0-7368-6025-8 (hardcover)
    1. Signs and signboards—Juvenile literature. I Title: Señales y rótulos. II. Title.
HF5841.B3818 2006b
338.3'122—dc22   2005054155

Written by David Bauer
Developed by Raindrop Publishing

Editorial Director: Mary Lindeen
Editor: Jennifer VanVoorst
Photo Researcher: Wanda Winch
Adapted Translations: Gloria Ramos
Spanish Language Consultants: Jesús Cervantes, Anita Constantino
Conversion Assistants: Jenny Marks, Laura Manthe

Photo Credits
Cover: Cris Pedegral Martin; Title Page: Gary Sundermeyer/Capstone Press;
Page 4: David Crawford/Image Farm; Page 6: Gary Sundermeyer/Capstone Press;
Page 8: Gary Sundermeyer/Capstone Press; Page 10: Gary Sundermeyer/Capstone Press;
Page 12: Gary Sundermeyer/Capstone Press; Page 14: Gary Sundermeyer/
Capstone Press; Page 16: Image Farm

1 2 3 4 5 6 11 10 09 08 07 06

Signs
by David Bauer

Señales y rótulos
por David Bauer

Yellow
Umbrella
Books
for early readers

A street sign.

Es una señal
de ceder el paso.

A stop sign.

Es una señal de alto.

A sidewalk sign.

Es un rótulo portable.

SORRY WE'RE

OPEN TO SERVE YOU ➡

BUSINESS HOURS	
MON.	9 a.m.-5 p.m.
TUE.	8 a.m.-6 p.m.
WED.	8 a.m.-6 p.m.
THU.	8 a.m.-6 p.m.
FRI.	8 a.m.-6 p.m.
SAT.	12 p.m.-5 p.m.
SUN	CLOSED

A store sign.

Es un rótulo público.

A bike sign.

Es una señal de bicicleta.

A train sign.

Es una señal de tren.

A duck sign!

Es una señal
de cruce de patitos.

Index

Índice